Machines with Power!

Tractors

by Amy McDonald

BELLWETHER MEDIA
MINNEAPOLIS, MN

Blastoff! Beginners are developed by literacy experts and educators to meet the needs of early readers. These engaging informational texts support young children as they begin reading about their world. Through simple language and high frequency words paired with crisp, colorful photos, Blastoff! Beginners launch young readers into the universe of independent reading.

Blastoff! Universe ★

Reading Level — Grade K

Grades 1-3

Grade 4

Sight Words in This Book 🔍

a	in	on	what
are	is	the	
do	it	them	
have	make	there	
help	many	they	
his	of	this	

This edition first published in 2021 by Bellwether Media, Inc.

No part of this publication may be reproduced in whole or in part without written permission of the publisher. For information regarding permission, write to Bellwether Media, Inc., Attention: Permissions Department, 6012 Blue Circle Drive, Minnetonka, MN 55343.

Library of Congress Cataloging-in-Publication Data

LC record for Tractors available at https://lccn.loc.gov/2020007067

Text copyright © 2021 by Bellwether Media, Inc. BLASTOFF! BEGINNERS and associated logos are trademarks and/or registered trademarks of Bellwether Media, Inc.

Editor: Christina Leaf   Designer: Andrea Schneider

Printed in the United States of America, North Mankato, MN.

Table of Contents

What Are Tractors?

What is in
the field?
A farmer
on his tractor!

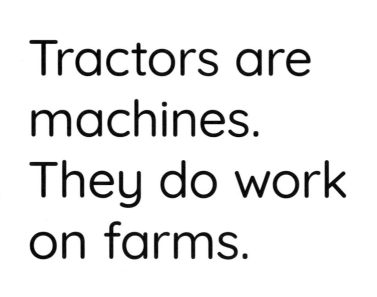

Tractors are machines. They do work on farms.

Parts of a Tractor

Tractors have an **engine**. It makes them move.

engine

Tractors have
tall wheels.
They drive
over land.

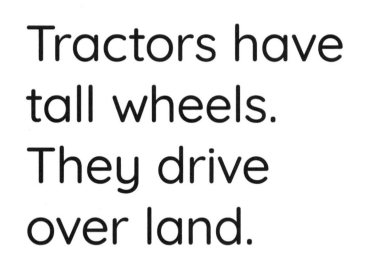

wheels

Tractors have
a **hitch**.
It pulls tools.

hitch

tool

There are many
kinds of tools.
They help
farmers do work.

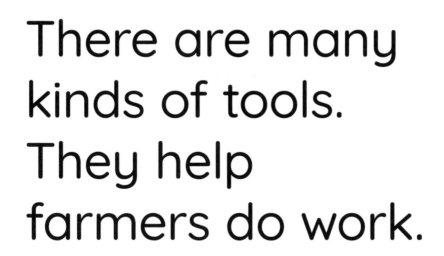

box blade

tiller

loader

15

This tractor pulls
a **box blade**.
It makes land flat.

box blade

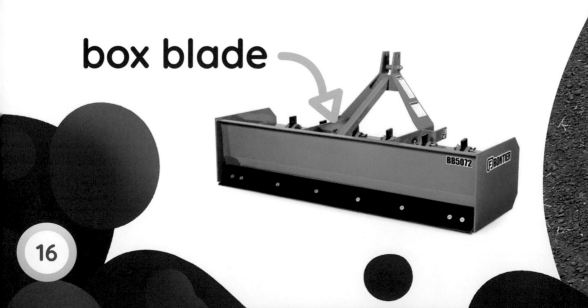

This tractor
pulls a **tiller**.
It digs in the dirt.

tiller

This tractor
lifts hay.
It works hard!

Tractor Facts

Tractor Parts

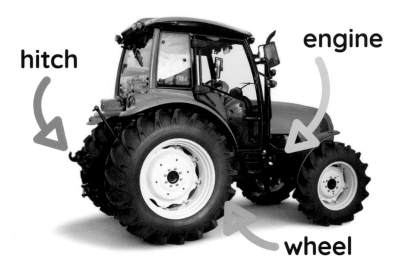

hitch

engine

wheel

Tractor Tools

box blade

tiller

loader

Glossary

box blade

a tool with a
wide, flat edge

engine

the part that
makes a
tractor go

hitch

a part that
hooks tools
to tractors

tiller

a tool that digs
in the dirt

To Learn More

ON THE WEB

FACTSURFER

Factsurfer.com gives you a safe, fun way to find more information.

1. Go to www.factsurfer.com.

2. Enter "tractors" into the search box and click .

3. Select your book cover to see a list of related content.

Index